Original title:
Tropical Moments

Copyright © 2025 Creative Arts Management OÜ
All rights reserved.

Author: Seraphina Caldwell
ISBN HARDBACK: 978-1-80581-624-9
ISBN PAPERBACK: 978-1-80581-151-0
ISBN EBOOK: 978-1-80581-624-9

Sweet Symphony of Sunrise

A parrot screams, it's way too loud,
Sunlight spills, a golden shroud.
Birds in chorus, off-key tunes,
Dance with shadows under balloons.

Coffee cups spill, a comical sight,
A palm tree leans in sheer delight.
Laughter echoes, waves join in,
Nature's giggles, where do I begin?

Velvet Nights with Nocturnal Whispers

Stars wink down, wearing shades of gold,
Crickets chatter, secrets unfold.
A coconut falls, thumps on my head,
In this comedy, I'm lightly fed.

Glow worms twinkle, like disco balls,
A turtle waltzes, as night falls.
Laughing with shadows that slide and sway,
As moonlight giggles and leads the way.

Sun-Kissed Dreams and Coral Currents

Surfers tumble, riding foam and cheer,
Sand sticks to toes, oh dear, oh dear!
A beach ball flops up high in the air,
And splashes down, without a care.

Fish in flip-flops swim with glee,
Waving hello, "Come join me!"
Laughter bubbles from the shore,
As sea turtles play and dance for more.

Captured Moments in Paradise

Snapshots clicked with silly poses,
A toe in the sand, where laughter flows.
My hat blows off, a seagull's prank,
I dive for it, oh, how I sank!

Mango juice dribbles down my chin,
A messy victory, oh what a win!
Together we giggle, moments shared,
In this paradise, we're unprepared.

Chronicles of the Cascading Isles

In the shade of a giant palm,
A coconut fell with a thud,
I chuckled, 'Oh dear, that's alarming!'
As it rolled off down to the mud.

The crabs in their little ballet,
Seemed to strut with a diva's flair,
While I tried to play it all okay,
But ended up stuck in a chair!

A parrot whispered secrets, it seems,
While I munched on a fruity delight,
'You should really follow your dreams!'
But they all seemed to take flight.

Then a flamboyant toucan appeared,
Swooping low with a wild caw,
I laughed as my worries disappeared,
What's next, an iguana with a straw?

In the dance of that sparkling tide,
Waves giggled as they came to play,
With a splash here and a slide wide,
Every moment felt like a bouquet.

Blossom and Tide: A Convergence

The waves wear a funny hat,
As shells dance a jig on the mat.
Flowers laugh in the sunny glow,
While crabs do the cha-cha, oh so slow.

Seagulls squawk in a silly tune,
As jellyfish float like balloons in June.
The palm trees sway with a wink so sly,
Inviting all to give it a try.

The Canvas of Coastal Colors

Paintbrushes dipped in sunshine gold,
Dancing with laughter, unafraid, bold.
Flip-flops snap with a jolly beat,
As sandcastles rise, so mighty and neat.

Crabs wearing sunglasses stroll the shore,
While waves play peek-a-boo, oh what a score!
Bathers splash in vibrant delight,
Chasing seagulls that swoop with a fright.

Glistening Sands and Gentle Breezes

The sand tickles toes with a teasing touch,
While kites dive and dance, oh so much!
Laughter bubbles like soda pop,
As flip-flops fly, and the fun won't stop.

The sun grins wide in a beach ball race,
With sunscreen applied, just in case!
A beach bum naps, snoring out loud,
While hermit crabs boast to each other, proud.

Serenity Found in Swaying Hammocks

Hammocks swing like laughter's embrace,
As pineapples wear a spiky face.
Coconuts giggle, rolling away,
While sunsets paint skies in a goofy display.

A llama in shades joins the fun,
As island tunes twirl 'round like a bun.
Chasing fireflies, so smooth and slick,
In this cheerful moment, we dance and kick.

The Harmony of Horizon and Sea

Beneath the sky so blue and bright,
A seagull steals my sandwich light.
The waves hum tunes of silly glee,
As crabs dance like they own the sea.

My flip-flops flop with every step,
A crab just waved, oh, what a rep!
The sun blinks down, a cheeky tease,
While I chase shadows of the breeze.

Cascading Waterfalls and Sweet Frangipani

Water tumbles with a joyful splash,
The fish all giggle, make a dash.
Frangipanis sway, a fragrant show,
While frogs on leaves put on a row.

A monkey snickers, swings nearby,
"Oh no!" I shout, as I slip and fly!
Falling petals land on my nose,
As laughter bubbles, and the fun grows.

Lull of the Lagoon at Dusk

The sun dips low, paints skies with fire,
A raccoon steals snacks, oh, how dire!
The lagoon whispers silly dreams,
As dolphins plot their laughter schemes.

A boat floats by, with giggles galore,
The captain's hat now floats ashore!
As night approaches, stars all twinkle,
The sea critters share jokes that crinkle.

Everchanging Tides of Tranquility

The tide comes in, oh what a race,
A beach ball bounces, lands on my face!
The playful waves invite us near,
As shells reveal their secret cheer.

Sandcastles crumble, oh what a scene,
A seagull swipes my ice cream!
In this fluid dance, we twist and shout,
With laughter echoing all about.

Moonlit Tides

Under the moon, crabs start to dance,
Flip-flops fly in a sandy romance.
Seagulls squawk, what a funny sound,
Waves giggle as they splash all around.

A starfish claimed my beach chair,
Waving its arms without a care.
I offered it snacks, a feast for a king,
It just gave a shrug, no joy in that bling!

Laughter echoes as coconuts fall,
A cannonball splash, oh, what a brawl!
My buddy slipped, slid right on the shore,
Rolling like a fish, now who's keeping score?

When the tides rise high, and the sunset's bright,
We're all just goofballs, holding on tight.
A night of mischief, under the stars,
Sharing our giggles, no need for guitars.

Henna and Sunsets

Henna's swirling on a hand so fair,
Then it rained, oh what a scare!
Patterns ran, turned into a mess,
I laughed so hard, couldn't care less.

Golden skies with a twist of pink,
Dancing seahorses make me rethink.
Should I paint my toenails in lime?
But what if I slip? Quite the fun crime!

Friends all gathered near a barbecue flame,
But someone burnt the hotdog, oh what a shame!
Instead of dinner, we feasted on fries,
While the sunset painted the world in surprise.

With henna hands and silly grins,
We juked and jived, letting the fun begin.
Under the laughter of the twilight's glow,
We ended the night with a silly show!

The Color of Paradise

In the color splash of the sunset hue,
A parrot squawked, 'Is that lime or is that blue?'
Salty air laughs with every breeze,
Coconut drinks, oh, such silly tease!

Flip-flops flying, a dance on the sand,
A sandcastle battle, oh isn't it grand?
Someone's bucket, lost in the tide,
While we're all trying not to slide!

Laughing at fish that always seem shy,
They dart away, not one for the pie.
We're just like them, in this vibrant chase,
Finding joy in every little space.

We painted smiles on our sunburned cheeks,
Sharing stories of love and sneaky peaks.
In the color of paradise, our laughter remains,
Together forever, like those silly waves' gains.

Sweet Island Breeze

A breeze comes whistling with a cheeky grin,
Sandy toes playing, let the fun begin!
We chase the laughter, rolling on the ground,
While our beach ball bounces, round and round.

Someone tried surfing, balance was key,
But fell in the water, splashing like a pea!
Riding the waves with giggles galore,
Nothing's as fun as a splash and a roar.

Tropical fruit, a taste of delight,
But the pineapple dance? A comical sight!
Juices are flowing, sticky and sweet,
Our laughter echoes, can't take a seat.

As we wave goodbye to the setting sun,
With footprints behind, oh what fun we've spun!
The island breeze carries tales of our play,
In our hearts forever, like bright holiday.

Joy Beneath the Coconut Tree

In the shade of a leafy crown,
A squirrel danced in a coconut gown.
He juggled fruits, he made a fuss,
While I sipped juice, oh what a plus!

A monkey swung with a silly grin,
Slipping on shells, a comic win.
He threw me a coconut, what a game,
I tossed it back—oh, what a shame!

With laughter echoing through the air,
We shared a joke, without a care.
The sun would wink, the breeze would tease,
Joy flourished here, just like the trees.

So if you find a nutty spree,
Come join the fun beneath the tree.
For here we laugh, we joke, we play,
In nature's circle, full of sway.

The Pulse of the Sea

Waves that dance like silly fish,
Swirling around our sandy dish.
A dolphin laughed, did a flip,
Right next to me, it made me trip!

Seagulls squawked, oh what a noise,
Chasing after a kid's lost toys.
I threw my hat into the tide,
It came back soaked, but I felt pride!

Buckets built with castles high,
Waves came crashing, oh my, oh my!
With each splash, a giggle arose,
The ocean's pulse, it surely knows.

So here we play, with sand and sea,
Making wishes, wild and free.
Laughter echoes with salty cheer,
Moments of joy, always near.

Swaying Palms and Sunset Dreams

Palms that swing like they're in a dance,
With my drink in hand, I took a chance.
I tried to waltz, but tripped on roots,
Yet even that brought giggles and hoots!

The sunset painted the sky in gold,
As I spotted a crab being bold.
It tried to steal my tasty snack,
I chased it off, but just got whacked!

With friends around, the jokes would flow,
A sunburned nose, an awkward show.
We reminisced of silly things,
Like the time I wore a crown of strings!

So raise a glass to the setting sun,
For silly moments are all in fun.
With swaying palms and dreams in sight,
We'll laugh and play until the night.

Whispering Waves and Golden Horizons

Waves whisper secrets to the shore,
I strayed too close, now I'm galore!
With wet feet and giggles loud,
Every splash felt like a proud crowd.

A crab waved at me, oh what a sight,
I waved back, feeling quite light.
It scuttled away with a snappy snap,
I just stood there, in a beachy flap!

The sun dipped low, a fiery ball,
I tripped on sand, but didn't fall.
Friends laughed hard, our voices bright,
In this golden glow, everything's right.

With every wave, a playful tease,
We danced to the rhythm of the sea breeze.
So let's celebrate this life we own,
In laughter and joy, we've truly grown.

In the Shade of the Banyan Tree

Under branches wide, we hide,
Sipping drinks with floating ice.
Lizards tease from trunks, they glide,
While squirrels plot their grand heist.

A picnic spread, a wild affair,
Sandwiches stacked high, we cheer.
But ants march in with perfect care,
Bureaucratic of the picnic sphere.

The sunbeams dance like a wild jive,
In coconut hats, we all cheer loud.
We swear the bugs have come alive,
To join our feast, so well endowed.

But as we laugh, one misstep stalls,
A sandwich lands on a lizard's face.
He gives us looks that speak of brawls,
As we all burst in fits of grace.

Aromas of Algae and Adventure

At the beach, we find our spot,
With snacks that smell like ocean lore.
A wind gust swirls, the paper's caught,
And chips are flying, oh, what a score!

A wave approaches with a roar,
Our cooler sails off to sea.
We chase it down, a funny chore,
But instead, we're soaked with glee.

The gooey algae clings like glue,
A game of tag turned into muck.
With laughter contagion, we all flew,
As splashes warred, abandoned luck.

Eventually, we find our prize,
A soggy sandwich and old fries!
Through fits of giggles, no surprise,
In goopy times, we wear our highs!

Voices of the Wildflower Beach

Seagulls squawk a beachy tune,
While sandcastles rise like dreams.
We laugh and sing beneath the moon,
In flip-flops gone rogue, it seems.

Wildflowers bloom, a colorful mess,
Bees buzzing in a joyful dance.
We try to share, but what a stress,
They favor nectar, not the prance.

As kites fly high, we lose our grip,
On laughter as they start to dive.
Catching wind, let's take that trip,
To where silliness is alive!

Finally, a bonfire's glow,
We toast marshmallows, all in row.
The smoke is thick, but hearts aglow,
In coziness, our bonds will grow.

Swimming in Celestial Light

In pools that shimmer, we all float,
With rubber ducks, we sail away.
Sun-kissed skin on a rowdy boat,
Getting splashed is part of the play.

A jump from high, a belly flop,
The splash zone's wide, a laughing crowd.
A friend calls out, "You'll never stop!"
In waterworks, we're feeling proud.

The lifeguard watches, not impressed,
As cannonballs create a storm.
But we embrace the childlike jest,
While mermaids dodge and freeform swarm.

In evening glow, the stars appear,
We skyward glance and chuckle tight.
For in this space, there's none to fear,
We swim through laughter, pure delight.

The Allure of Azure Waters

The waves giggle and tease,
As I dodge the splashes with ease.
A seagull steals my sandwich,
Oh, what a beakish wrench!

Floating on a giant raft,
I tried to paddle, made them laugh.
Endless sunburn, what a sight,
Yet I wear my tone with delight.

The sunbeam smiles down on me,
Sipping coconut juice with glee.
But when I try to take a sip,
It splashes all and makes me slip!

Sand in my shorts, oh dear me,
The price you pay for sea-fried glee.
But in this paradise so bright,
Even mischief feels just right!

Traces of the Mango Moon

Beneath the moon's soft, sticky glow,
Mango slices steal the show.
I trip over my sandy toes,
Chasing fireflies, oh how it glows!

The night air buzzes with sweet glee,
While I belt out tunes like a bee.
Coconut shells clink in my hand,
We're dancing like a wobbly band.

I drop my drink, it splashes wide,
Sticky laughter can't subside.
As fruit flies join this wacky dance,
I vow I'll fix my fruit mischance!

Yet the mango moon, it smiles bright,
Winking at our silly flight.
In this balmy, absurd spree,
Life's a laugh that's wild and free!

Canvas of Currents

Brushstrokes of waves in a playful mood,
My beach ball flies—oh! A lucky dude.
But then it bounces off a sunbather,
Chaos rolls in like a mischief creator!

Painting seashells no one can decipher,
I try to sketch but my grip is ciphered.
My brush takes a dip in the azure hue,
And suddenly, it's a modern art zoo!

The seagulls squawk like they own the show,
Snatching snacks from the folks down below.
They swipe my snack, quite rude and brash,
Yet I laugh and watch as they dash!

Currents of fun in every turn,
With sandy feet, my heart will yearn.
For every giggle, splash, and swirl,
In this whimsical watery world!

At the Edge of the Emerald Sea

A pirate hat on my soggy head,
Searching for gold but finding bread.
Oh wait! It's just a piece from lunch,
But the gulls, they laugh, ready to munch!

I try to build a fortress tall,
But each wave giggles, says, 'Not at all!'
As sandy towers crumble down,
I declare I'm the sandcastle clown!

On floaties, we race, I take the lead,
Then boom! I'm tangled like a weed.
Shouts of joy, we burst with cheer,
As the lifeguard waves with a goofy leer!

In this land where silliness roams,
We find our joy in the ocean's domes.
The emerald waves, they beckon me,
And I answer with a carefree spree!

Maritime Moods and Melodies

Seagulls sing on salted breeze,
Fishermen dance with shaky knees.
Their nets are tangled, what a sight!
Caught more seaweed than fish tonight!

A crab in sneakers tries to race,
With flippers on, he sets the pace.
He'll win the prize for best dressed Crust,
But eats his trophy, that's a must!

Boys on boards just try to glide,
But wipeouts send them to the tide.
They laugh and shake the water clear,
"Next time, let's skip that front flip, dear!"

The sunset paints the sky with flair,
As mermaids giggle, tossing hair.
With jokes and jests, the night takes flight,
Life's punchlines land just right tonight.

Dance of the Hibiscus

Hibiscus sways in cheeky glee,
Swinging with bees, oh what a spree!
Petals twirl like they're in a show,
"Careful now, don't steal the glow!"

Palm trees gossip, swaying low,
"Look at that sunburn! Oh no, whoa!"
Fronds wave like they're fans in a crowd,
As sunbathers yell, "I'm so proud!"

A lizard strikes a funky pose,
Doing the cha-cha on his toes.
"Is that a dance, or just a scare?"
"Call it art, with sun in my hair!"

Breezes tease with playful hints,
Tropical laughter increases spins.
Let's toss confetti made of sand,
With every twirl, we'll make a stand.

Echoes of the Ocean's Heart

Waves are giggling, splashing free,
"Did you hear that?" says the sea.
Whales are telling fishy tales,
Of shipwrecks and old treasure trails!

Clams hold meetings on the shore,
Discussing pearls and ocean lore.
They sport their shells, they strut and pose,
Hoping to catch sunbathers' oohs!

Dolphins leap in synchronized bliss,
"Let's learn this dance, you can't miss!"
They twist and turn with sparkling grace,
While surfers wipe out at their pace!

Seashells whisper silly secrets,
As sea stars share their best regrets.
The rhythm of laughter fills the air,
In ocean's heart, we're always rare.

Sunlit Shores and Serene Skies

Under sunbeams, shenanigans fly,
A toucan asks, "Hey, you got a tie?"
As flip-flops flop, and laughter ensues,
Sandcastles stand, with goofy views!

Children chase the waves with glee,
"Catch me, I'm faster!" shouts the spree.
But salty splashes and hectic rolls,
Turn beach days into joyous scrolls!

A picnic spreads, oh what a sight,
With sandwiches flying, what a flight!
Ants march in for a tiny feast,
While seagulls hover, looking for least!

As the sun dips, shadows grow long,
We sing our laughter, it feels so strong.
In these moments, smiles ignite,
Under skies where everything's bright.

Secrets of the Cove

In a cove where campfires glow,
The crabs have started a show.
They dance with glee, so wild and free,
While the seagulls squawk in a row.

A coconut fell, oh what a sight,
It rolled away, what a funny flight!
Fish giggle too, in bubbles they play,
As waves crash with all their might.

With flip-flops lost, we stumble around,
Searching low, high, and underground.
A parrot squawks, 'You'll never find,
Your shoes, my friend, are lost, unbound!'

In this nook, laughter is key,
Splashing water just for tea.
We sip on joy from a pineapple cup,
And toast to life with wild esprit!

Rainforest Reverie

In the jungle where monkeys swing,
They learn to salsa—they do the fling!
A toucan squawks, 'Hey, don't be shy!'
While leaves fall like confetti in spring.

The iguana struts in a cool hat,
Saying, 'Look at me, what do you think of that?'
While frogs serenade with a croaky tune,
And a sloth sways by, just as flat.

A butterfly joins the dance of the day,
Spinning and twirling, what a display!
While we laugh at how we can't keep pace,
As the jungle sings, come what may.

Under the canopy, we've found our groove,
Making memories, oh how we move!
With wildflower crowns and hearts so light,
In this lush world, we truly improve!

The Ocean's Lullaby

Waves lap softly like a gentle hand,
While starfish gather to make a band.
They strum on shells, it's quite absurd,
With a octopus composing—oh isn't it grand?

A jellyfish floats with a jelly-like grin,
Joining the music with a squishy spin.
The dolphins laugh, leap, and dive,
Making us wonder, who let them in?

Seagulls squawk, trying to sing too,
But their voices squeak, and sounds go askew.
They honor the waves, with clumsy flair,
Watching the tide, in a comedic view.

As the sun dips low, colors take flight,
With laughter echoing into the night.
The ocean hums with stories untold,
As we sway together, oh what a delight!

Swaying Shadows

In the twilight, shadows dance and twirl,
Palm fronds sway, as the night does unfurl.
A firefly winks, like it knows a joke,
While lizards play tag, giving it a whirl.

The moon peeks out, a cheeky grin,
While the crickets chirp, 'Let the fun begin!'
A monkey swings by, takes a dramatic fall,
And lands with a plop; oh where to begin?

We share silly tales, with laughter so loud,
While the wind joins in, feeling so proud.
Every rustle, a giggle, in the night so bright,
Creating mischief, in a lively crowd.

As the stars blink down, we revel in cheer,
Awash in the joy that's crystal clear.
Under swaying shadows, we find our delight,
In the magic of moments that linger near.

The Enchantment of Exotic Isles

A parrot perched, with dazzling flair,
Whispers secrets in salty air.
Sandcastles wobble, their builders laugh,
As crabs attempt a sneaky path.

Coconuts drop, a thud on the sand,
While beachgoers dance in a conga band.
A sunburnt tourist, in shades so bright,
Can't find his towel, oh what a sight!

Flip-flops flop on the ocean's beat,
Seagulls squawk in a feathered heat.
With mango smoothies, they toast the sun,
In goofy hats, life's just more fun!

In vivid sunsets, laughter's the key,
As friends dive headfirst into the sea.
A jellyfish floats with grace and cheer,
As we giggle at a nearby deer.

Journey through the Caribbean Breeze

Swaying palms in an island song,
A deck chair sways—oh, not for long!
With sunscreen smears, they turn and twist,
While sipping drinks, they can't resist.

Fishermen cast tales with lines galore,
On boats with names like 'Catch Some More.'
A dolphin jumps, making quite a splash,
While sunbathers watch, hoping for cash.

Rum punch spills like a fruity surprise,
As someone spots a crab in disguise.
Limbo contests draw a crowd, oh my!
Who'd thought bending could make you fly?

Snorkelers dive into blues so bright,
Searching for treasures, a curious sight.
With fins too big, they wobble and spin,
Chasing fish while trying to grin.

Soft Echoes of Evening Bliss

As twilight falls, the sky's a canvas,
A firefly's dance, a tiny fiesta.
With laughter echoing through the palm trees,
They toast to the night, in a buzzing breeze.

Marshmallows roast over a flickering flame,
Someone's s'mores take on a life of fame.
A misplaced bite, sticky hands galore,
They giggle at faces, sugar-crusted and more.

A guitar strums under stars that twinkle,
As off-tune voices begin to crinkle.
Frogs join in with their ribbiting rhyme,
Nature's chorus, tirelessly sublime.

In this island moment, joy can't be bought,
With stories woven from laughter caught.
While waves whisper secrets to the shore,
The night goes wild, who could ask for more?

Dreams on a Driftwood Shore

On driftwood loungers, the world feels right,
A crab marches by, it's quite a sight.
With sunglasses high, and goofy grins,
Life's a game where we all just win.

The sea breeze tickles, what fluffy hair,
As fish throw kisses without a care.
In inflatable flamingos, they float with glee,
While someone splashes, declaring, "Look at me!"

A sandman stands, he's six feet tall,
But a seagull swoops, now he's nothing at all.
Laughter erupts at each silly feat,
With victories grand, each moment sweet.

As shadows stretch, the fun won't end,
With tales to tell, and new ones to send.
Beneath the stars, they make a wish or four,
On this driftwood shore, who could want more?

Paradise Found

In the shade of leafy trees,
I sip my drink with a tease.
A coconut falls on my head,
Now I'm dreaming of my bed.

Sandy toes and a sunburned nose,
A seagull steals my snack, it goes!
Laughing loud, I chase it down,
In my flip-flops, I almost drown.

The fish are swimming, what a show,
But tripping over seaweed, oh no!
My snorkel's leaking, water flies,
At least I got a funny prize!

As the sunset paints the sky,
A crab waves me goodbye.
With laughter ringing in the air,
Paradise found, without a care.

Waves of Wonder

The waves dance like a silly clown,
In my beach hat, I flop around.
Caught in a splash, I tumble deep,
Now the fish know my secret, I can't keep!

Surfboards lining up in row,
An octopus says, "Don't go slow!"
It pulls me under with a wink,
I pop back up and start to think.

My sunscreen bottles fight for space,
Sticky and mad, what a funny race!
I slathered it everywhere, oh dear,
Now I'm a glimmering souvenir!

As the tide pulls back with a laugh,
I might just need a life raft.
Yet here I am, so full of glee,
Waves of wonder, wild and free.

Echoes Under the Palm

Beneath the palms, I start to sway,
The wind whispers jokes all day.
A lizard makes a comic face,
While I try to find my place.

The hammock swings, a joyful ride,
But I flip out, oh what a slide!
The crabs just chuckle, what a sight,
As I giggle and hold on tight.

Bright parrots squawk in silly tunes,
Dancing under the silver moons.
They mimic my laugh, quite the prank,
"Is that a joke?" I say, "Give thanks!"

Time flies by, as I savor,
Every funny, silly flavor.
Echoes under the palm, you see,
Life's a joke, and laughs are free!

Sun-Kissed Memories

Sun-kissed skin and a bright smile,
I'm here to laugh and stay awhile.
A beach ball bounces right on cue,
Smacking my friend, oh what a view!

Ice cream drips like a funny story,
Sticky hands tell my little glory.
The gulls are cawing their set list loud,
And I'm dancing, feeling proud.

Someone's sunburned like a lobster,
But they're still out, our goofy roaster.
A tale of laughs and sweet delights,
Under blazing, starry nights.

So let the waves keep rolling in,
With each laugh, let the fun begin.
Sun-kissed memories all around,
In this joyful paradise found.

A Saltwater Serenade

The seagull's squawk is quite a treat,
It steals my chips, then takes a seat.
With sandy toes and sun-kissed nose,
I laugh at life as the ocean flows.

A crab scuttles by in a hurried dance,
I mimic him, but with no chance.
The breeze plays tricks with my straw hat,
It flies away—now where's that cat?

The waves crash down with a splishy splash,
I try to dodge, but it's a mad dash.
With every tumble, a giggle escapes,
As fish play tag in their sea-shaped capes.

I gather shells along the shore,
But seashells seem to roll and snore.
In this wild world of beachy fun,
I'll trade my worries for rays from the sun.

Reflections in the Tidal Pool

I peek inside the pool so clear,
And see my face, oh dear, oh dear!
A fish swims past with a curious glance,
While I just wave and lose my pants.

The starfish grins, it seems to know,
That I'm the star of this beachy show.
I slip and slide on a seaweed trail,
My laughter echoes, a joyous wail.

The tide rolls in with a cheeky grin,
I splash around, let the fun begin.
The crabs throw parties, clapping their claws,
While I try to dance, forgetting decorum laws.

Each sudden wave brings laughter loud,
As I find myself lost in the crowd.
Reflecting joy in salty pools,
Where giggles reign and laughter rules.

Harboring Happiness in Every Wave

I spot a dolphin, flipping high,
He greets me with a wink and a sigh.
I try to mimic, flailing about,
He just dives down—what's that about?

Seashells sing in the warm sun's rays,
Each unique note sets my heart ablaze.
In search of treasure, I trip and fall,
With laughter echoing, I know it all.

The beach ball rolls like it's got a mind,
It dances past, leaving me behind.
As I give chase on this sandy race,
I find myself with a seagull's grace.

With every wave, joy slips away,
But comes right back—what a silly play!
In this harbor, with sun-kissed days,
Happiness lives in the ocean's ways.

Luminous Mornings and Fading Light

The sunrise greets with golden beams,
I stretch and yawn, still lost in dreams.
A crab's parade steals my morning gaze,
Life's a circus amidst ocean spray.

Seashells scatter in the morning glow,
Each one whispering secrets below.
I pick one up, it smirks with pride,
Did it just wink? I must decide.

As the sun dips low, shadows creep,
The waves say goodnight, softly they sweep.
I laugh with friends by the firelight,
Trading stories of this day's delight.

With coconut drinks and laughter sweet,
The stars emerge, a nightly treat.
In this land where joy takes flight,
Each fading moment is pure delight.

The Language of Laughter in Known Shores

On sunlit sands we spill our drink,
With salty jokes that make us blink.
The seagulls squawk, they mock our fun,
As laughter dances, one by one.

The crabs join in, with sideways strut,
They make us laugh, they raise the cut.
Between the waves and sun-kissed skin,
Our silly tales will always win.

A breeze comes in, it tickles toes,
We giggle loud, as sandbag blows.
In every wave, a chuckle brews,
With each splash, our joy renews.

So let's toast to this sea-bound jest,
Where every wave has laughter blessed.
With colorful drinks and stories shared,
In this great ocean, we're all declared.

Harmonies of Hummingbirds and Plumeria

In gardens bright, the birds do flit,
With tiny feet on flowers sit.
Their buzzing songs, a comical hum,
Each bloom they tease, they can't be glum.

Plumeria sways, giggles in breeze,
As honey drips with such sweet ease.
The birds a dance, in swift parade,
Mix nectar with each laugh they made.

"Watch me zoom!" the hummingbirds say,
As petals swirl in breezy play.
They tease the breeze with flitty grace,
In floral realms, we find our place.

So join the fun, come take your part,
The garden's laughter warms the heart.
With humming sounds and colors bright,
Our silly joy takes joyous flight.

A Dance in the Tropical Dusk

As daylight fades, the fireflies gleam,
In a shimmering glow, we start to beam.
The moon winks down, "Let's have a ball!"
With laughter loud, we heed the call.

We twirl and spin on the cool, soft grass,
With giggles that echo, as good times pass.
The crickets chirp their evening tune,
While shadows join our dance 'neath the moon.

A coconut drops; we all jump high,
With hearty laughs, we touch the sky.
The stars above, they wink and shake,
At our silly steps, their glow they break.

So swing your partner, take a chance,
This dusk invites spontaneous dance.
In laughter's embrace, let worries fly,
Under the watch of the moonlit sky.

Coastal Whispers and Enchanted Journeys

With ocean whispers, we set our sails,
On cardboard boats, with made-up tales.
The waves giggle, as they splash our feet,
With every bump, the laughter's sweet.

A salty breeze messes up our hair,
We shout, "Look at us, no time to care!"
Seagulls swoop in, like they own the place,
Our snacks they steal, with comical grace.

From beach to shore, a race we start,
But trip on sand, we fall apart.
The sun dips low, a painted scene,
As giggles echo, we're kings and queens.

So here's to journeys with friends galore,
Where every laugh opens a door.
In coastal air and ocean's sway,
Our hearts stay light, come join the play!

Island Whispers

Sandy toes in my flip-flops,
Clams play hide and seek, oh, what a flop!
Crabs dance sideways, quite the show,
I dropped my drink, but hey, let it flow.

Seagulls squawk, stealing my fries,
I shout, "Hey bird! Don't be so sly!"
With sunburned skin, my hat's askew,
But who needs style when the sky's so blue?

Coconut hats on the beach patrol,
Sipping coconut water from a hole,
My buddy tripped on a beach ball,
Laughter erupts, we're having a ball.

A hammock swayed in the balmy night,
Pretend I'm a pirate, ready to fight,
As stars blink down on our silly spree,
Cheers to the moments, just you and me!

Sunlit Serenade

Sunshine wrapped in a hammock's hold,
I sunbathed wrong, now I'm bright gold.
The lifeguard's whistle, a comical sound,
"Don't dive into the sand!" he astounds.

Buffet tables of colorful treats,
So many snacks, I'm tripping on sweets.
Watch out for the pudding, it's a big mess,
I blame the seagulls for all my distress.

Beach games like tug-of-war with ice,
The loser is wet, and not once, but thrice.
A splash here, a laugh there, such delight,
Until the sun sets, we party all night.

Singing with sandals, feet in the sea,
Maybe I'm a mermaid, you should agree.
With silly jokes, we greet the dawn,
Sunkissed and giggling, we carry on!

Palms in the Breeze

Palms sway to a rhythm of waves,
A conga line forms, mischief it braves.
Flip-flops clapping, we dance with glee,
Oh dear, did someone step on my knee?

Barbecue smoke and the scent of fun,
The cook is dancing, he's on the run.
Hotdogs fly as we cheer in delight,
Don't forget the sunscreen, it's quite a sight!

Splashing water, it's a riotous scene,
We took a selfie, but someone's unseen.
I aim to pose, but a wave rushes in,
And now it's just splashes and hearty chagrin.

As the sun sets, we sing away night,
With ukuleles, we find our light.
Belly laughs echo, under starry skies,
Our beach shenanigans just never die!

Laughter on the Shore

Waves tickle toes, we scamper and squeal,
Sand castles crumble, oh, what a deal!
Seashells for treasures, we hunt with delight,
It's a mermaid's competition tonight.

Seagulls steal snacks, it's quite the affair,
Chasing them off, it's beyond compare.
Ice creams melt faster than we can scoop,
Sticky fingers make us a goofy troupe.

We ride the waves, surfboards in hand,
Sometimes we tumble, like we had planned.
With every splash, we erupt with laughter,
Creating stories we'll cherish thereafter.

As twilight falls, and the stars amuse,
We toast marshmallows, our own little cruise.
Starlit giggles and moonlit beams,
Life by the ocean feeds our dreams!

Lush Canopy Adventures

Swinging through the vines, I trip and fall,
A parrot squawks, 'Dear human, watch the wall!'
Monkeys laugh as I tangle in my clothes,
While ants throw parties, nobody knows!

Zip lines zoom as I scream in delight,
A squirrel sneezes, causing quite the fright.
Mother nature giggles, I'm losing my cool,
Dancing leaves whisper, 'This is the rule!'

Jungles teem with joy, the sun begins to hide,
A sloth says, 'Why rush? Take a long ride!'
With each clumsy step, I find a new game,
A sign says, 'Welcome to the mishap fame!'

So here I swing on this humorous raid,
Even the flowers seem unafraid.
In the lush green vista, I find my peace,
Laughing with nature never seems to cease.

Serenity by the Shore

Seagulls dance, but I trip on my feet,
Spilling my drink, oh isn't that sweet?
The sunset winks, as waves start to play,
While my hat flies off, it seems to sway!

Shells in hand, I search for treasure,
But find a flip flop, oh, what a pleasure!
The water tickles, it's sure to tease,
As a crab scuttles by, trying to please.

The breeze plays pranks, the towels take flight,
Barefoot adventures lead to delight.
With each splash and laugh, the day fades away,
Serenity wraps up, come what may!

With the moonlight's glow, the night starts to hum,
I dream of tomorrow, with more silly fun.
On sandy shores, joyful hearts will soar,
Forever finding laughs and giggles galore!

Breezy Blossoms

Petals flying like confetti in glee,
A bumblebee buzzes, takes aim at me!
With each gentle breeze comes a silly whirl,
As I spin and twirl, my hair's a swirl!

Butterflies flutter, they tease and they sway,
'You've got pollen!' they giggle, 'Hey, hey!'
In this floral frolic, laughter is rife,
A loopy dance in this blooming life.

Wobbling through gardens, I stumble and fall,
But blossoms all around cushion it all.
A thistle says, 'Be careful, my friend!'
As my laughter echoes around every bend!

In breezy blossoms, with scents that arise,
I learn to embrace each surprise that flies.
Nature's humor, forever at play,
In this floral circus, I want to stay!

Fisherman's Twilight

At dusk, the fishing line tangles with glee,
As I reel in a boot, not a fish, you see!
The moonlight twinkles on waters so wide,
While a fish flips and flops, oh my, what a ride!

Lures and laughter dance on the boat,
A sea gull shouts, 'That's the wrong kind of moat!'
With bait in one hand and snacks in the other,
I chase a catfish, yelling, 'Come hither, brother!'

Waves crash softly, but I splash like a child,
Casting nets and hooks, I must seem quite wild.
The stars wink down, they share in the fun,
A catch of the day? Not yet, but I've won!

As twilight winds down, tied up in my mess,
With fish tales to tell, life's a humorous fest.
Glancing at my sunset, I can't help but smirk,
In the twilight laughter, my heart finds its perk!

Vibrant Echoes of the Tropics

In a hammock tied tight, a bird flew by,
With a squawk and a twitch, it said hi!
I spilled my drink, it landed on my hat,
Now I'm a walking joke, how about that?

The sun plays hide and seek with my shade,
While crabs dance sideways, they've got it made!
A parrot laughs loud, it's the life of the show,
While I'm busy tripping over my own toe.

Coconuts roll like they're in a race,
All while I'm trying to keep up the pace.
The beach bum next door is building a throne,
But really it's just a pile of sand and phone.

With friends all around, the laughter takes flight,
How can a misstep make everything right?
So raise your glass high, let's toast to the fun,
In our funny paradise, the day's just begun!

Celestial Waves and Starry Nights

The moon is a disco ball in the sky,
With waves dancing up, they can't even lie.
I tried to surf, but fell face-first with a splash,
Now fish are my friends, they're having a bash.

Stars twinkle bright like they're sharing a jest,
While I'm busy counting, they put me to test.
A crab with a wink says, "You've got no style!"
I wave back and giggle, it's been a while.

The sandcastles sway, they're giants, you see,
As I stumble and laugh, oh where could I be?
Nights filled with giggles, and complaints from the seas,
Even the dolphins are rolling with ease.

So here's to the nights where we all find our vibe,
In the golden glow, we feel so alive!
With waves and some jokes, let the fun take its flight,
Until morning arrives to chase off the night.

Rhythms of Reef and Reflection

With fins like a dance and bubbles in sight,
I dove in the reef, what a wondrous delight!
A turtle named Fred swam up, made a grin,
"You've got sand in your hair and a shell for a skin!"

The vibrant fish winked with a splash and a flip,
While I fumbled my snorkel, almost took a sip.
A clownfish chuckled, "You think you're so sly,"
But my mask wouldn't fit, what a comical lie!

The corals held secrets and whispers of life,
But all I could hear was the sound of my strife.
I emerged from the waves with seaweed as a crown,
A true underwater jester in my ocean gown!

So here's to the laughter that bubbles below,
In this silly dance, let the good vibes overflow!
With rhythms of nature, each splash brings delight,
As we swim with our smiles, it just feels so right!

Nature's Palette at Day's End

As the sun dips low, it paints the skies wide,
With hues that are laughter, our joyful guide.
I tripped on a flip-flop, did a silly dance,
While butterflies giggled, taking their chance.

Palm trees waving, looking chic and quite bold,
While I'm trying to balance on a table of gold.
A coconut drink spills, it's a slippery mess,
But that only sparks more giggling, I confess!

Fireflies begin, putting on quite a show,
As I fumbled my phone, oh, where did it go?
Friends gather 'round, and we toast to the light,
With wishes of chuckles that twinkle all night.

So here at the end, with colors we blend,
Every joke, every spill, they simply transcend.
Let's cherish each smile as the day says farewell,
With stories of laughter, magic, and swell!

Scented Serenades in the Jungle

In the jungle where the monkeys swing,
The flowers burst, their fragrances cling.
A parrot squawks a tune so bright,
While ants do the cha-cha through the night.

Coconut falls with a thud and a roll,
While a monkey takes a header, what a goal!
Lemurs argue over the best fruit treat,
As a sloth just lounges, mellow on the beat.

A jaguar naps on a sunlit rock,
Dreams of disco under the tick-tock.
Vines twist and twirl in a silly dance,
While beetles bask in a bug's romance.

Laughter echoes through the leafy maze,
As critters join in for the wild craze.
With every twist and turn that they make,
The jungle sings of joy, no mistake!

Echoes of the Undercurrent

Beneath the waves, a fish named Fred,
Wears a goofy grin and a bright pink head.
He tries to surf on a bubble wave,
While a crab gives chase, oh how he misbehaves!

A dolphin giggles, flips through the tide,
With seaweed wigs, they take pride.
A stingray glides, taking a bow,
As a clam gets stuck, oh how will it wow?

The starfish claps, what a grand display,
As seahorses prance, hip-hip-hooray!
Instead of a show, they dropped their cue,
And danced a jig, oh it's true, it's true!

In this watery world, where the laughter flows,
Creatures unite in their silly shows.
An octopus tries to juggle some shells,
And the sea, it giggles, oh can you tell?

Dancing Shadows on Shimmering Sand

On the beach where the sunbeams flicker,
Little crabs scuttle, oh they're quite the quicker.
They bump and tumble with a cheeky cheer,
As surfers wipe out, let out a cheer!

A seagull swoops by with a chip in tow,
While a tourist shouts, 'Watch out below!'
Coconuts roll like they're in a race,
A sandy foot chase puts smiles on each face.

Umbrellas sway and laughter rolls,
As kids build castles with sticky goals.
A wave crashes down, splashing all around,
With squeaky sandals, we twirl on the ground.

Beneath the sun's warm, golden light,
Joyful shadows play, oh what a sight!
Each moment wraps in a giggling twist,
In a dance of shenanigans, no fun is missed!

Silhouettes against a Painted Sky

As the sun dips low, the horizon glows,
With flamingos posing, striking their shows.
They march with style, like a runway cheer,
While a sunset painter swigs coconut beer!

Bamboo shakes with the breeze on the sand,
Where kids with ice-cream make art so grand.
A dog runs by, the ice cream's no more,
As children laugh, what a messy encore!

The sky paints colors, a pastel delight,
While sun-kissed cheeks glow in fading light.
A kite comes loose, oh what a surprise,
It flies in circles, 'round clueless guys!

As laughter echoes and silhouettes sway,
Under the splendor of a twilight play.
Each joyful moment, with friends nearby,
Makes memories linger, oh me, oh my!

Driftwood Tales on the Shoreline

A log waves hello, it seems to smile,
Its wooden grin stretches a mile.
Seagulls gossip about the driftwood's chat,
While crabs scuttle past, wearing a hat.

The tide pulls back, the stories unfold,
Of sunburnt tourists and treasures untold.
Sandcastles crumbling, their reign is brief,
Captured by waves, then gone like a thief.

A starfish whispers with a secret tease,
'I'm not a fish; I just go with the breeze.'
The beach is a stage, full of quirky delight,
Where every seashell has something to write.

So come build your dreams on this shoreline bright,
With driftwood and laughter, from morning to night.
The whispers of waves are a comical tune,
In the comedy club of the sunny afternoon.

Lapping Lyrics of Lagoon Waves

The lagoon sings softly, a bubbly refrain,
As fish do the cha-cha, much to my disdain.
Flamboyant seaweed dances with glee,
While crabs sip their coconut - oh, what a spree!

The sun takes a dive in a pastel sky,
And the turtles nodding, as if to comply.
Water lilies giggle, floating on dreams,
While frogs croak their songs in harmonious themes.

The breeze twirls like a dancer, so spry,
Tickling the waves as they leap by.
A pelican swoops, in a crash, it's unclear,
If it's capturing fish or just spreading cheer!

Oh, laughter rides high on the crest of each wave,
In this lagoon, perfect for those who are brave.
Join in the fun, let your worries all float,
In the lap of these lyrics, just rock and just gloat.

Paradise Painted in Pastels

In colors so bright, the sand is a dream,
Sunsets are artists, or so it would seem.
A canvas of laughter splashed with delight,
Where surfboards and smiles take off in the night.

A parrot recounts tales in pastel hues,
Of penguins in sunglasses sipping fruit brews.
The pineapple hats are quite all the rage,
As monkeys all prance from their leafy stage.

The sunflowers giggle, tilting their heads,
While sand dunes whisper secrets to beds.
In this playful paradise, joy is the law,
Where the only offense is forgetting to draw.

So bring out your crayons, let's color the sky,
Create masterpieces as clouds float on by.
In a land where the funny feels perfectly real,
A haven of fun is the best kind of deal.

A Breeze Through Coconut Canopies

The coconut trees sway, all in a dance,
While monkeys caricature their luck and chance.
With every gust, their leaves play a tune,
Of cheeky adventures beneath the soft moon.

The breeze carries laughter, like candy on air,
As toucans gossip without a care.
'What's with that cat?' a gecko now quips,
'He's trying to surf on a wave with no flips!'

The coconuts chuckle, they bob in delight,
'We're softer than pillows, try sleeping all night!'
With tales of vacations, so silly, so bright,
The canopy whispers 'join in the rite!'

So lounge in the shade, let the jungle unfold,
Be merry, be silly, be playful, be bold.
In this mix of laughter and sweet tropical cheer,
A breeze through the branches brings friends ever near.

Nautical Nights and Moonlit Vistas

Sailing on a squeaky boat,
With a parrot that won't gloat.
Slipping on a jellyfish,
Oops! That wasn't my wish!

Stars giggle in the sky,
As the seagulls fly awry.
A crab dances on the shore,
To a tune we can't ignore.

Waves growing merry and bold,
As stories of fish are told.
Bright lanterns flicker and sway,
Is dinner served? We can't stay!

A splash and laugh break the night,
With tangled nets and fishy bite.
Onward to the rocky beach,
Where sunset's colors loudly preach.

Whispered Secrets Beneath the Palms

Palms gossip in the breeze,
About the antics of the bees.
A coconut drops like a drum,
Oh, watch out! Here they come!

Squirrels plotting a grand theft,
While sunbathers just feel bereft.
Someone's hat flies like a kite,
Oh dear! It took a flight!

Laughter floats among the fronds,
As kids play tricks with their wands.
A monkey swings, a playful tease,
Should we hide the fruit with ease?

Secrets whispered, giggles swell,
With stories we'll surely tell.
Underneath the leafy shade,
While funny memories are made.

Refreshing Rains and Radiant Rays

Raindrops dance on my umbrella,
While I sip on cold vanilla.
A rainbow sprinkles in the mist,
And puddles start a water twist.

Sunshine peeks with a bright smile,
As umbrellas dance in style.
Flip-flops squelch, creating sound,
Oh my! That's a funny pound!

Chasing the clouds, kids must run,
Their laughter shines like the sun.
Splashing friends with joyful cheer,
Is it summer or a fair?

With sun and rain as our friends,
This fun will never end.
Capture the moments of play,
In this silly, sunlit sway.

A Conch Shell's Timeless Song

A conch shell blows a whiny tune,
As dolphins dance under the moon.
Listen close, you might just laugh,
As crabs try to join the staff!

Seashells scatter, a jazzy beat,
Oh wait! Was that a fish's feat?
Giggles echo as they swing,
When clams start up their bling bling!

Turtles stroll with a swagger,
While starfish cheer and do a stagger.
The seaweed waves, it's time to play,
In this underwater ballet!

A melody of waves unfurl,
As all the sea critters twirl.
With laughter that sings, we embrace,
The whimsy of this oceanside space.

Waves of Serenity

I tried to surf on a giant wave,
But landed instead in a seaweed cave.
The fish laughed hard, they saw me flail,
As I shouted, 'Help! I've turned into a snail!'

Seagulls squawked, their own jokes to share,
While I danced clumsily without a care.
The sun was bright, my sunscreen a thrill,
But who knew sand could cause such a spill!

With each wave, I got lost in my thoughts,
About crab competitions and dancing hotshots.
I left my worries somewhere on the shore,
Joined a conch shell chorus and wanted more.

In the end, I rode the waves with glee,
A seaweed dance was the sight to see.
So here's to laughter amidst the tides,
In this silly play where joy abides.

Mango Dreams

In a market where mangoes tease my sight,
I grabbed one, took a juicy bite.
Suddenly the pit went flying wide,
And a hungry parrot swooped with pride!

Fluffy clouds decided to play peek,
As I chased the mango that flew like a streak.
Bumping into llamas and ducks in a row,
They quacked at my folly, 'What a show!'

I slipped on some juice, oh what a mess,
Laughter echoed, I must confess.
The sun shined bright over fruits gallore,
While my belly tickled, I wanted more.

Every mango tells a tale to unfold,
With sweet laughter and stories bold.
So here's to mishaps with a fruit so fine,
In this sunny world, it's simply divine!

Saltwater Reflections

Staring into the waves with a grin,
I saw my reflection—but wait, there's a fin!
A fish winked at me, what a cheeky guy,
Then flipped and swam off, oh me, oh my!

I waved hello to the crabs on the shore,
One waved back; they've got moves galore.
They sassed and danced on the sandy ground,
While I tripped over my towel, oh what a sound!

A splash here, a giggle there, oh what fun,
I chased jellybeans, oh aren't they a run!
With salt in my hair and smiles galore,
I felt like a child, forever wanting more.

So what if I fell? It's a part of the game,
In this water ballet, we all share the fame.
And every splash brings a laugh that connects,
In this salty life, joy never defects!

The Dance of Hibiscus

Hibiscus blooms with a wink and a twirl,
They invited me over, so I gave it a whirl.
A flower party under the sun's rays,
I tried to salsa, but ended in a gaze!

The petals giggled as I made a fuss,
While bees joined in, oh what a plus!
With pollen shoes on, I tapped my feet,
But stepped on a slug—oh, what a treat!

Dancing with flowers isn't quite normal,
Yet these silly blooms made me feel formal.
So we spun around, twirling with grace,
While a cheeky lizard hopped in my space.

At the end of the day, with laughter abound,
We bloomed with joy, all twirling around.
With each petal's dance, I'll cherish this go,
In the garden of life, let the fun always flow!

www.ingramcontent.com/pod-product-compliance
Lightning Source LLC
Chambersburg PA
CBHW072131070526
44585CB00016B/1632